BEAUTIFUL BIRDS

MINDFULNESS MEDITATION
ADULT
COLORING BOOK

ASSEMBLED BY
MADDIE MAYFAIR

ISBN-13: 978-1540819161

ISBN-10: 1540819167

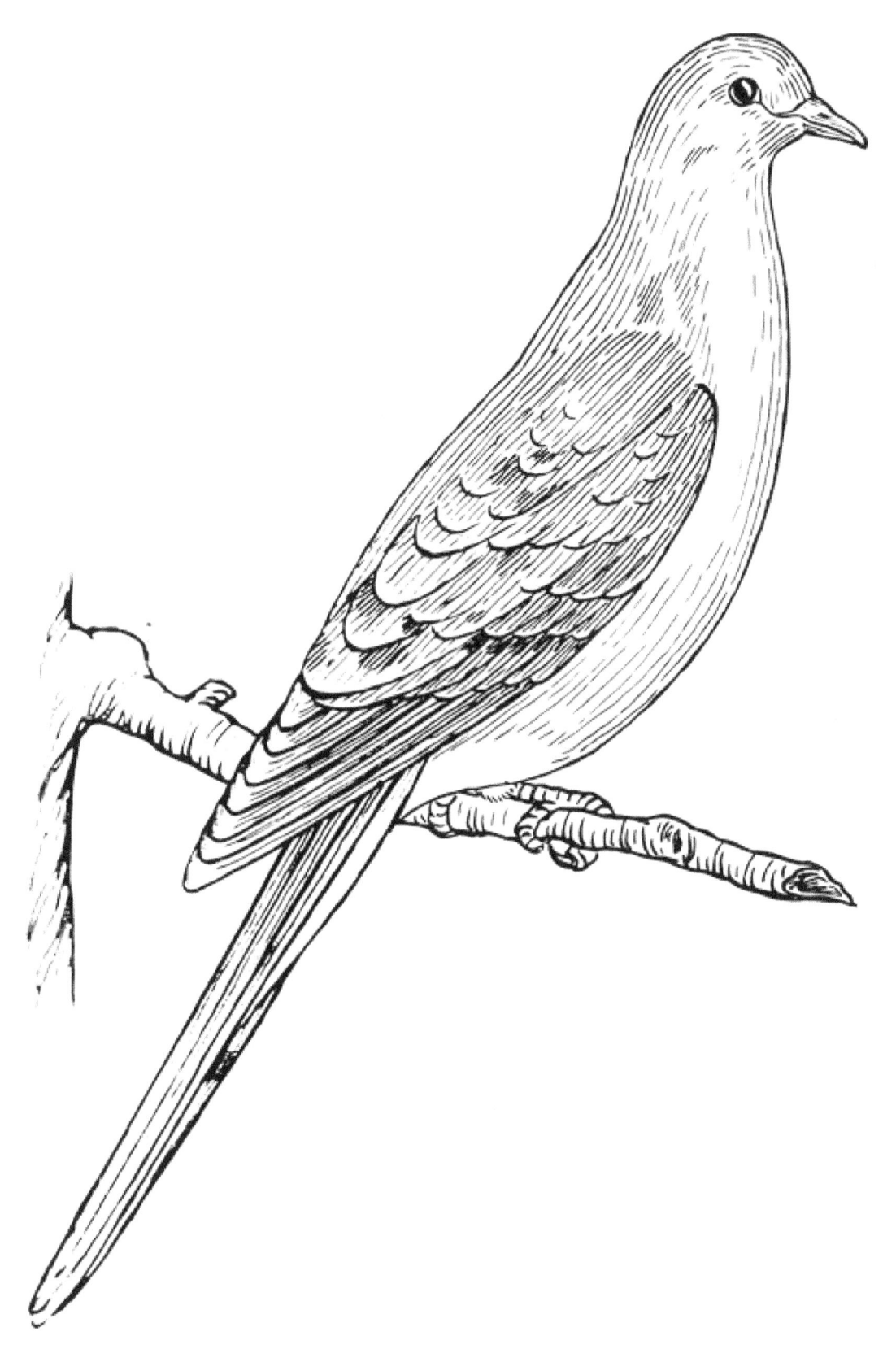

Enjoy even more *Colouring Books for Grown-Ups,* including:

www.ingramcontent.com/pod-product-compliance
Lightning Source LLC
Chambersburg PA
CBHW081757280526
45789CB00008B/2899